FLORENCE NIGHTINGALE

by Pam Brown

OTHER TITLES IN THE SERIES

Marie Curie by Beverley Birch (1-85015-092-3)
Father Damien by Pam Brown (1-85015-084-2)
Henry Dunant by Pam Brown (1-85015-106-7)
Mahatma Gandhi by Michael Nicholson (1-85015-091-5)
Bob Geldof by Charlotte Gray (1-85015-085-0)
Martin Luther King by Valerie Schloredt and Pam Brown
  (1-85015-086-9)
Mother Teresa by Pam Brown (1-85015-093-1)
Raoul Wallenberg by Michael Nicholson and David Winner
  (1-85015-109-1)
Coming Soon
Albert Schweitzer by James Bentley (1-85015-114-8)
Sir Peter Scott by Julia Courtney (1-85015-108-3)
Desmond Tutu by David Winner (1-85015-087-7)
Lech Walesa by Josef Kamensky (1-85015-107-5)

Picture Credits
J. Bethell: 11 (below); Bridgeman Art Library: 12, 24, 50, Forbes Collection 13, 33 (above), Giraudon 17, Royal Holloway College 54, Victoria & Albert Museum 33 (below); City Art Gallery, Manchester: 31; Mary Evans Picture Library: 34; Fine Art Photographic Library: 4; Fotomas Index: cover, 23, 24 (below), 44 (below); GLC Photo Library: 10, 9, 35, 36, 41 (left), 46, 57 (top), 59; Illustrated London News: 11, 28, 32, 38, 52; Mansell Collection: 14, 15, 18, 29, 44 (left); National Army Museum: 40 (top), 42; National Portrait Gallery: 8, 16, 43; National Trust: 8, 57 (below, both); Royal Collections, reproduced by gracious permission of Her Majesty the Queen: 30; Royal College of Nursing 41 (right); George Weidenfeld & Nicholson Ltd: 20; Welcome Medical Museum: 40 (below); Zefa Picture Library: 48.

Maps drawn by Geoffrey Pleasance.

Published in Great Britain in 1988 by
Exley Publications Ltd
16 Chalk Hill, Watford, Herts WD1 4BN, United Kingdom.

Copyright © Exley Publications Ltd, 1988

British Library Cataloguing in Publication Data

Brown, Pam
        Florence Nightingale———(People who have helped the world).
        1. Medicine. Nursing. Nightingale, Florence, 1820-1910.
        Biographies. For children.
        I. Title
        II. Series
        610.73'092'4

ISBN 1-85015-117-2

Series conceived and edited by Helen Exley.
Picture research: Kate Duffy.
Research: Diana Briscoe.
Editorial: Gail Jarrett and Margaret Montgomery.

Printed and bound in Hungary.

FLORENCE NIGHTINGALE

The tough British campaigner who was the founder of modern nursing

Pam Brown

The Nightingales abroad

The great coach lurched as the six sweating horses reached the top of the pass, but these Italian roads were nothing to those the family had met in France and Papa barely looked up from his book of Greek verse. Mama, swathed in rugs and half asleep, stirred drowsily but without alarm. Florence stared out into the gathering dusk while her sister, Parthenope, continued to sulk.

It was the February of 1838 and the Nightingales were exploring Europe. The carriage was roomy enough inside to accommodate nine or ten people and fitted out with little innovations to add to their general comfort. The servants sat on the roof, but whenever the views were spectacular and the weather kind, they were joined by Florence and her sister.

However large the carriage, the appalling roads and the flea-ridden inns meant such journeys were still a great adventure and needed both stamina and courage. But the Nightingales had enjoyed themselves hugely, especially Florence, whose diary was bursting with the excitement of all that she had experienced since leaving England the previous September. It had all been such a wonderful contrast to life at home ... "like an Arabian Nights dream come true".

Despite the busy life that the family had in England, caught up in the activities of innumerable cousins and aunts and uncles, Florence found her existence there wearisome. At eighteen she was pretty and clever – far more so than her rather resentful sister, Parthenope – but Florence was a strange mixture of clear-headedness and over-sensitivity. She all too early retreated into fantasies she knew were in danger of taking over her whole life.

Opposite: Florence Nightingale was born into a wealthy family. She would never have been expected to earn a living. The whole family could afford to travel around Europe for seven months at a time with their own carriage and six servants. The Nightingales' coach was grander than the one in this picture. It held eleven people, with all their luggage, and was drawn by six horses. (Painting by Heywood Hardy)

Parthenope, or Parthe as she was known, was a year older and far more like their extrovert mama than their studious father. She did not enjoy the long hours of lessons in Greek, Latin, German, French, History and Philosophy imposed by Mr. Nightingale. She was even more aggravated by the fact that Flo not only enjoyed them, but excelled in every subject.

When they had reached Nice, on the south coast of France, where many English people lived, Florence was swept away in a passion for balls and dancing. Genoa, further along the coast in Italy, she liked even better. It was an exciting city and there were more balls, more concerts and operas, and splendid sights to see – and more very amiable young men to admire the two sisters. Especially Florence. She was "much noticed". Now the city of Florence lay ahead, the place where she had been born on May 12, 1820.

It was to prove even more beautiful and exciting than she had hoped. The past seemed as alive as the present – everywhere magnificent palaces and churches, everywhere paintings and statues almost as alive as the fashionably-dressed people who had come so far to admire them. And music. The city seemed to be brimming with music – and Florence was "music mad".

The balls eclipsed all that had gone before. Florence, caught up in the music and gaiety, danced till dawn. The winter went by in a flurry of visits and dances and opera-going – a swirl of silks and lace, of concerts and music. And with the spring came outdoor fetes and dancing under the fresh green of the trees.

A woman of two minds

After a summer tour of the beautiful Italian lakes, the family moved on to Geneva in Switzerland. The city was full of political refugees and Florence began to learn about a world totally different from the one she had so far inhabited. It was one of poverty, hardship, courage and determination. That part of her that had fought against fantasies and

Parthenope and Flo. Demure and ladylike young ladies of breeding filled their time before marriage with reading, music and embroidery, with perhaps a discreet visit to some deserving poor family on the estate. Florence wanted more – far, far more. She was appalled by the uselessness of many wealthy women's lives.

longed for the challenge of reality seemed to come to the surface.

She had loved the fun and excitement and beauty, but there was another part of her that demanded discipline and order. Her diaries were full of enthusiasm, and they were meticulously kept, listing times, dates, distances and careful observations of all that had caught her interest.

Among the details of receptions, dances, vistas and paintings, were notes concerning the plight of the poor. The fun and frivolity had not blinded her to the misery of the people living in areas that had been touched by war. She had been taken to Europe to learn – and she had learned about much more than dancing, music, opera, paintings and fine architecture.

Florence, through all those long months of travel,

A very proficient sketch by Parthenope of Embley House, the Nightingales' country home in Hampshire. Living in such affluence in beautiful parkland and flower gardens, it would have been easy for Florence to shut her eyes to the world of poverty and suffering beyond the park gates.

Opposite: This portrait of the young Florence reading by the window of Lea Hurst, one of the Nightingales' gracious homes. Flo looks a very subdued daughter of the house, with no hint of the turmoil in her mind. But she was already both widely and deeply read.

had had a secret – a secret that was to shape her entire life.

On February 7, 1837, she had written in a private note "God spoke to me and called me to His service". From that day on Florence was convinced that one day it would be clear to her, and that when it was she must obey, however hard the task turned out to be. She was sure that there was some special purpose for her life. But sixteen years were to pass before her life changed to one of service.

The shadow of home

At first the return to England in 1839 seemed to make no great change to Florence's way of life. Her parents were unaware of her inner torment and the Nightingales divided their time between their two country homes and London. Those who met Florence were struck by her vivid good looks, her beautiful shining chestnut hair, her grace and her wit. She was full of life, clever, admired and caught up in a summer of laughter and dancing. Henry Nicholson, the brother of her best friend, Marianne, wanted to marry Florence and Marianne was doing everything in her power to persuade Florence to accept. Her mother, Fanny, had great hopes for her – a brilliant marriage, a country estate and a house in London, perhaps even success as a great hostess. Florence had put her "call" out of her mind. At times she almost forgot it. But as the year

9

A rare, early photograph of Florence Nightingale. When she escaped from her family, she dressed more simply, turning her back on the fashionable society of her childhood.

went on, the memory of it began to haunt her.

Young well-brought-up ladies of her time were expected to be quiet, genteel, respectably religious and busy with small concerns. Servants did the work, the men of the house went out into the wide world to pursue their professions – and there was little or no hope of a lady taking up any real career.

Yet it was seen as acceptable that working class women should slave away in the heat and noise of factories from dawn to dusk, that they should be employed in the terrible, back-breaking work of chain making, that they should be forced into prostitution because the work of sewing rich ladies' clothes or rich men's shirts paid so little.

But the well-to-do women often suffered too, in a different way. Their lives were narrow, boring and useless. Most men were very nervous indeed about women with opinions, much less ambitions. A handful succeeded as writers or painters – but even they often had great difficulties to overcome. Ladies were supposed to marry well, to raise families and to be submissive and supportive wives.

But Florence was an educated, thinking, concerned human being and she felt she was suffocating among the teacups and potted ferns, the polite conversations and the endless, endless evenings sitting around the fire on the many occasions when there were no invitations to dine or dance. Florence felt like screaming the house down, but she bit her tongue, and became more and more depressed. Inevitably she became physically unwell. The family packed her off to stay with her Aunt Mai in London. More socializing, not less, was, they felt, a certain cure for such inexplicable gloom.

Queen Victoria was about to marry her adored Albert, and Flo seemed to share in the excitement. She appeared to everyone to be much better; no one could see her despair. She felt she was filling her days with silly, useless things. Part of her could still get pleasure from them, but underneath the consciousness of time passing, of time wasted, gnawed at her. Was her life to go on like this forever?

While Florence longed for a chance to work to do something that was useful, the vast majority of women lived in poverty. Unlike Florence they were forced to work long, long hours for a pittance.

Mathematics

Desperate for something positive to do, Florence took up the study of mathematics. It gave her weary, confused mind something to focus on, something clear and precise and disciplined. Aunt Mai understood her need. "Flo and I have been getting up at 6, lighting a fire and sitting very comfortably at our work," she wrote to Fanny. "And I think if she had a subject which required *all* her powers and which she pursued regularly and vigorously for a couple of hours she would be happier all day for it."

But her mother, Fanny, did not approve. Florence's destiny, in her firm opinion, was to marry well and to become the head of a household. What use was mathematics in such a circumstance? Even the intellectual Mr. Nightingale thought history or philosophy would be more sensible and relevant.

But Flo was beginning to develop the stubborn streak that was to be her salvation. She stuck to mathematics.

FANNY SMITH
(Mrs. NIGHTINGALE)

Fanny Nightingale, Florence's mother, never understood Florence's dream of helping other people. She enjoyed the social side of life.

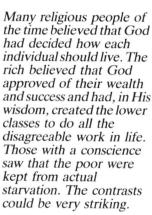

Many religious people of the time believed that God had decided how each individual should live. The rich believed that God approved of their wealth and success and had, in His wisdom, created the lower classes to do all the disagreeable work in life. Those with a conscience saw that the poor were kept from actual starvation. The contrasts could be very striking.

It was no use. She was soon back home, where she grew more and more miserable. She struggled to continue her studies on her own. Up in her bedroom she read Greek and Philosophy and Mathematics, working in the cold, early hours before the rest of the household was awake.

She felt she was drowning in small things, her time consumed by countless small tasks. She was only twenty-two and as an unmarried girl was at everyone's beck and call. It was her duty to make herself useful. She was always busy, but somehow busy doing nothing of any real value. Her life seemed pointless to her, to be leading nowhere.

Waking up

Florence lived at a time when there was a great chasm between the rich and the poor.

Unlike many well-off people of her time, Florence did not shut her eyes to all this misery. During the summers at one of the Nightingales' country homes, she had visited the poor with soup and money. Now she looked at the dinner tables of the

well-to-do: they were weighed down with food. She looked at the wealthy women frittering away their lives: they were wearing dresses that had been sewn by starving girls who stitched away all day and then by candlelight through the night.

She wrote, "My mind is absorbed with the idea of the sufferings of man ... I can hardly see anything else. All the people I see are eaten up with care or poverty or disease." She ached to be useful, but what could she do? Helping the real poor would not be considered proper.

Finding a mission

Then, in 1844, at the age of 24, she suddenly saw exactly what she could do. She could work in hospitals among the sick. Today that would seem a sensible and praiseworthy goal. Then it was absolutely impossible.

Hospitals were places to be afraid of, to do anything to avoid entering. They were dark, badly run, and dirty. Patients with all sorts of different diseases were crammed into the same ward, even the same

This oil painting shows Florence's social background. The men ran everything. Florence would be expected to look pretty and arrange flowers or sing. She couldn't even take an interest in cooking, because that was servants' work. Florence was one of the first women to break this vice-like mould. She said no to marriage and suffered greatly from the break with her family and with society. She paid a high personal price in order to have her own career.
(Painting by George Smith)

A cartoon of a sleeping, drunk nurse. Nurses had a very bad reputation at this time. They were regarded as uneducated and lazy – the dregs of society. With this image of nursing, one can begin to understand why Flo's family were alarmed at the prospect of her working in hospitals.

bed. It was not uncommon to see a man with a broken leg sharing his mattress with another patient who was dying of tuberculosis. The concept of hygiene was barely understood. The wooden floors of some hospitals were never scrubbed, the walls ran with damp and stank of fungus. Friends and relations of the patients smuggled in gin. The mattresses were sodden and the bedlinen was often not changed from one patient to the next.

Doctors did not wash their hands before surgery and wore their street clothes into the operating room, protecting them from splattered blood with the same grimy coat they'd worn to countless previous operations. Nurses, far from being angels of mercy, had a reputation for being drunken, careless, and dirty. People looked down on nurses – only the very worst sort of women worked in the squalor of hospitals. No lady could possibly be exposed to the sights and sounds of such places. Florence dared not even mention it to her family.

A first step

During the summer of 1844 an American Philanthropist, Dr. Samuel Howe, came to stay with the family and Florence asked him for advice – would it not be possible for a respectable woman like herself to be a nurse? Although it would be difficult, he thought "it would be a very good thing" and he encouraged her in her ambitions. A year went by and *still* she could find no way. Florence knew she *must* have training to be of any use and decided she would go to an infirmary to learn nursing.

Her mama was horrified, disgusted. Parthe had hysterics. Their Florence in a hospital? It was out of the question.

Flo begins to fight

By 1845 Florence was on the edge of complete despair. "I went down into the depths," she wrote. Despite pressure from her friends and family, she had refused the proposal of marriage from Henry

The Nurse — Old Style

Nicholson. She was determined now to follow her vocation. Secretly she began to study hospital reports – anything she could get hold of that would tell her about the way they were run and what was needed for their improvement. Long before dawn she would be at her desk, writing, writing, writing – begging friends for reports on German hospitals, French hospitals – every scrap of information she could gather.

At breakfast-time she smoothed her hair, put aside her papers and went downstairs to live the dull, monotonous life of the daughter of a well-to-do household. No one suspected her hidden life of study. Then, in October 1846, when she was twenty-six, a friend sent her information about an Institution of Deaconesses – ladies rather like nuns – at Kaiserswerth, in Germany, where respectable, religious women nursed the sick. It was a flicker of hope in the darkness. *Surely* her mother could not strongly object to her going to a place of such good reputation.

She dared not mention it yet. The strain of keeping up her hard, secret course of study and fighting down a deep despair was making her ill.

From the first day she walked into a hospital, Florence realized that the key to changing the hospital system was to make sure that nursing became reputable. In her lifetime, she transformed nursing into one of the most respected of all professions. She later wrote, "If a patient is cold, if a patient is feverish, if a patient is faint, if he is sick after taking food, if he has a bed sore, it is generally the fault not of the disease, but of the nursing."

Return to Rome

At the end of 1847, when Florence was twenty-seven, she had a nervous breakdown. Worried friends, Charles and Selina Bracebridge, whisked her away to Rome in the hope that the change would do her good.

The six months Florence spent there gave her back her health. They also gave her the friendship of Sidney Herbert, a man who in future years would be more important to her than any other – not because they would become involved romantically, but because they would do great work together.

Her time in Rome was not only pleasure. Florence managed to spend a lot of time at a happy, well-run orphanage and saw how such a place could and should be organized. As always, she made careful, thoughtful notes of what she had seen and learned.

But still, once she was home, she could discover no way of escape. Rome had been glorious, but it had solved none of her problems. Her mama and her sister continued to nag her incessantly. For the life of them they could not see why she did not accept and like their own way of life.

Sidney Herbert. Throughout his life, he was Florence's loyal friend and, as Secretary at War, would invite her to go out to organize nurses in the Crimean War. He literally worked himself into the grave in her service.

No to marriage

By 1849 she was deep in despair once more, and once more near suicide. She had not wanted to marry Marianne's brother – it had been no real hardship to refuse him. But now she felt deeply for another man, Richard Monckton Milnes, whom she'd met in 1842. He was intelligent and as Florence later said, "the man I adored".

But Florence knew now, more deeply than ever, that marriage could not be for her. To marry would prevent her from being of service.

By a tremendous effort of will, that summer she refused his offer of marriage.

It nearly broke her heart.

Her mother was absolutely furious.

Florence decided to visit Egypt with friends, and tried to take an educated interest in all she saw. She took notes and she read deeply, but it was as if only one part of her mind was so occupied. The rest was tormented by a sense of failure.

Her torment in Egypt had given her new determination. On July 31, she reached Kaiserswerth in Germany. The village pastor there had realized while touring around Europe that better nurses were needed. He had opened a local hospital, asking "Would not our young Christian women be able and willing to do Christian nursing?" Here, Florence was able to observe respectable religious women nursing the sick. She succeeded in staying for two weeks and left "feeling so brave as if nothing could ever vex me again".

It had been so short a stay, but what she saw inspired her to write a pamphlet on the work of the Kaiserswerth ladies. She wanted to persuade women like herself to take up similar work instead of wasting their days and their minds on tea parties and carriage drives.

She reached home on August 31, with Athena, her pet owl, safe in her pocket, and her heart high.

She was met by most bitter reproach.

"The Doctor for the Poor", a contemporary painting by J. Leonard. Enduring bad housing and long factory hours meant very serious health problems for the city people. It was work by men like this doctor that inspired Florence to give her life to help the poor.

Whenever she could, Florence would secretly visit hospitals. It was quite common to see two people in one bed. Patients with all kinds of diseases were crowded into dirty, disorganized wards. The smell was often so offensive that the hospitals had to be sprayed with perfume. Doctors would tour with handkerchiefs over their noses. Florence Nightingale would later write, pointedly, "The first requirement of a hospital is that it should do the sick no harm."

Parthe hurtled into her customary hysteria. Her mother, Fanny, stormed at Florence, telling her that she must never mention Kaiserswerth again and that she had disgraced the family. Perhaps she realized that, despite all her efforts, Florence was escaping her, and was not going to be the sort of daughter she wanted and expected her to be.

Six months of Parthe

Florence was a woman of thirty – and seemed no nearer her goal than when she had first heard her "call" at seventeen. All she wanted was her parents' permission to return to Kaiserswerth.

You would think that a grown woman, educated and respected, could have fought free. But this was 1850, not 1950, or 1990. In a middle class Victorian home any unmarried daughters were as much under their parents' thumbs as they were as small children.

Now things became worse, not better, for Florence. Parthe became more and more hysterical and ill. Papa and Mama declared that Florence was heartless and unfeeling to her dear, devoted sister. Florence had had a year on her own away from home, Parthe had had nothing. Her parents insisted that she make up for her year of selfish freedom by devoting herself completely to Parthe for the next six months. Florence, once again, gave in.

When her six months of slavery were over, Florence went immediately to stay with Sidney Herbert and his wife. The Herberts were sympathetic to her desire to break away from home and encouraged her in her ambition to become a nurse. Florence spent time with Dr. Elizabeth Blackwell, one of the first women ever to become a doctor. From Dr. Elizabeth, Florence learned that there was much a woman might achieve once she had made up her mind. She realized she had to take decisive action if she was to accomplish her own mission.

Her first step was accepting the fact that her family would never go along with her ambition. "I must expect no sympathy or help from them," she wrote in June 1851. "I have so long craved for their sympathy that I can hardly reconcile myself to this.... I have so long been treated as a child, and have so long allowed myself to be treated as a child."

Two weeks after writing this, plans were in place for Florence to return to Kaiserswerth. Although her parents forbade her to tell anyone exactly where she was going and why, they could no longer stop her. Her mother and sister went with her to Germany, pretending to the rest of the world that they were taking Florence for a three-month stay at the spa at Carlsbad.

Off to Kaiserswerth

Life there was hard. Food was simple and sparse. The students rose at 5:00 a.m. and meals lasted only ten minutes. The days were filled with frequent moments of prayer when everyone in a room got down on their knees and offered themselves to God. But Florence was happier than she had ever been in her life. She had escaped. At the age of thirty-one she was finally doing what she really wanted to do.

Full of a sense of self-esteem and purpose in life, Florence wrote one last beseeching, explanatory letter to her family. "Give me time, give me faith," she asked. "Trust me, help me.... Give me your blessing", she wrote. Her mother and sister made no reply. Florence never asked for their help or understanding again.

Cassandra

Florence returned from Kaiserswerth accompanied by her mother and sister. She was full of plans to learn nursing in earnest at a large London teaching hospital. But back home she found her father in severe pain with an eye ailment. He needed Florence to look after him and she felt she could not refuse. She had to go with her father on a trip to receive special treatment, but in a way their journey was a turning point. By the time they returned home, Mr. Nightingale was an ally in Florence's struggle against Parthe and her mother.

During this period Florence wrote an essay called "Cassandra". In the essay she described with great

"The late age of marriage, low marriage rates, wars and migration had created a pool of spinster labour. The single woman was prevented by powerful social pressures from competing in almost any field against the dominant male sex. If she did not marry, she must either remain at home to do the flowers, help her mother arrange tea-parties, or carry broth and jelly to the sick poor."
Madeleine Masson, from "A Pictorial History of Nursing".

"What is my business in this world and what have I done this fortnight? I have read 'Daughter at Home' to father and two chapters of Mackintosh, a volume of Sybil to Mamma. Learnt seven tunes by heart. Written various letters. Ridden with Papa. Paid eight visits. Done Company. And that is all."
Florence Nightingale, from her notebook, 1846.

An early photograph of . Florence. She was shy, modest and kind. But during the years of family conflict, she developed a steely determination that would help her in the years of campaign ahead.

bitterness a typical day in the life of the daughter of a prosperous Victorian family. "We can never pursue any object for a single two hours for we can never command any solitude," she complained. "And in social and domestic life one is bound, under pain of being thought sulky, to make a remark every two minutes."

Trapped again

Trapped in her family once more, the desperate Florence, a devout Protestant, asked the head of the Roman Catholic Church in England, Cardinal Manning, for advice. He suggested that even though she was a Protestant, her best hope was to go for nursing training at a hospital run by the Catholic Sisters of Charity in Paris.

England was a place of passionate religious loyalties and when Parthe and her mama heard of Florence's plan they went off into fresh and even more violent fits of hysteria.

Parthe's fits became so severe that she was taken to see the Queen's physician, Sir James Clark. In August 1852 he arranged for Parthe to go to his home in Scotland where she could be observed over some weeks. Dr. Clark soon reached a conclusion. He summoned Florence and explained that she must separate from Parthe, that, for her own good, Parthe had to learn to live on her own, without Florence. For her sister's sake, Florence would have to leave home.

Flo finds freedom

Florence had never realized before that every time she gave in to Parthe she was only making her worse. Now with Dr. Clark's advice she saw that it was better for everyone if she ignored Parthe's fits as much as possible and got on with her own life.

She decided to go to Paris, where she planned to stay at the hospital of the Catholic Sisters of Charity, dressing as a nun, but living separately from the sisters. Until then she had only one month to prepare herself.

All her pent-up energies came into action. She

visited hospitals, infirmaries, almshouses, institutions. She watched operations. She walked the wards with doctors and watched them examine patients with every kind of disease.

She circulated a questionnaire to French, German and English hospitals, comparing their answers and making notes and charts and lists. The knowledge that she had gained in those years of hidden study was of use at last. She had made herself an expert in her field – her gifts for order, research and decision-making were bearing fruit.

Florence's first job

In 1853 she accepted the post of Superintendent at the Institute for the Care of Sick Gentlewomen in Distressed Circumstances in London. She was employed to reorganize the institution completely. For the first time she would have a professional post where she could do the work for which her whole life had been a preparation.

The news plunged Mama and Parthe into a fresh bout of wild hysteria. They wailed, they wept, they reproached Flo, they refused to eat, they took to their beds. Papa moved out.

Flo shut her ears, and Papa, her new ally, decided to help her by granting her an allowance to enable her to be independent. His wife was furious.

Florence took her own rooms in London. The family objected, but she refused to give in. She was her own woman at last.

1 Harley Street

In August 1853, at the age of thirty-three, Florence Nightingale entered on her true career as Superintendent of the Institution for the Care of Sick Gentlewomen at 1 Harley Street, London.

It was as if those long, "lost" years suddenly burst into flower. Florence threw herself into the practicalities of organizing the hospital. She had just ten days to equip an empty house ready for patients to move in.

Hot water was piped to every floor. Lifts were put in to carry food up from the kitchens. A system

"The nurses did not as a general rule wash patients, they could never wash their feet – and it was with difficulty and only in great haste that they could have a drop of water, just to dab their hands and face. The beds on which the patients lay were dirty. It was common practice to put a patient into the same sheets used by the last occupant of the bed, and mattresses were generally of flock, sodden, and seldom, if ever, cleaned."

Florence Nightingale 1845 on a visit to a hospital.

21

of bells was installed, so that the patients could call the nurse on their floor.

The staff were rocked on their heels. Reorganization they had expected – but nothing like this. Florence was years ahead of Victorian thought in such matters – and her long endurance had taught her *not* to take no for an answer.

The committee was flabbergasted by these extraordinary demands and began to wonder if they had made a wise choice in Miss Nightingale. Florence quietly steam-rollered them into submission. She had the facts. She had the figures. It could be done. It must be done. Florence, released from the chains of family life, was proving to be a very formidable lady indeed. She never had vague ideas for improvements – she knew *exactly* how everything would work, how the bell system would function, how much coal was needed. She checked the larders. She checked the linen closets. No one could put over *anything* on Miss Nightingale.

Straight to the top

The treasurer refused to let her see the accounts every week. She made it *quite* clear that she expected them every week. She got them.

Nothing was too small for her attention. Out went rat-eaten bed-linen, out went soiled and stinking armchairs, out went rotted pillows. She acquired old curtains and transformed them into bedspreads. Quantities of brooms, brushes, and dusters were bought. Jam was made in the hospital's kitchens at a quarter of shop prices.

The committee reeled. So did the staff. Many were sacked or fled of their own accord. Florence installed a more efficient and hard working housekeeper. Her main problem was finding nurses who were properly trained.

It was incredibly hard work – she met with great opposition and had to make unpopular decisions, but she was wonderfully, remarkably happy.

Despite her efficiency she was well loved. She rubbed the feet of patients if she found them cold and she sympathized with women without hope or friends or money. She even sent some to the seaside to recuperate, at her own expense.

It was strange. She was a wonderful nurse – but there was a streak of coldness in her that frightened some people a little. It was as if the experiences of over-emotion she had had with her mother and Parthenope made her wary of softness. And softness was not going to make efficient hospitals. She needed to use her mind at its fullest stretch to reform them.

In a very short time, Florence was established as the specialist in her field, and work at 1 Harley Street was simply not enough to occupy her.

She prepared well-researched and well-presented papers on all manner of faults in the English hospital system. She was becoming more and more recognized as a leading authority.

Despite the ever-present objections of her family, Florence, wisely, stayed well away from them. She was no longer a puppet to respond to every twitch of the string. She had a job to do and she was going to do it. At the end of 1854 she drew up plans for recruiting farmers' daughters to be trained as nurses along the Kaiserswerth lines.

In a country where women had scarcely begun to fight free, Florence Nightingale was working as an equal with men.

In 1854, an outbreak of cholera swept through the London slums. Florence Nightingale volunteered to help and cared for filthy, terrified prostitutes and drunks with as much care as her sad patients at the Institute for Sick Gentlewomen. Florence held many of them in her arms while they died – there was little else she could do. Decades later, she would campaign for better sanitary conditions in the slums and London would never again be swept by cholera.

The Crimean War

Meanwhile all England was reading of the triumph of the British Army in the Crimea. Britain was fighting with France to support their Turkish allies in a war with Russia. Little did Florence know, as she read of the army's victories near Sebastopol, that she would soon be joining them. Not to fight the Russians, but to do battle with disease and the disorganization, filth and cold that went with it.

Florence Nightingale's experience, her intelligence, her courage and her determination were to be used to their very fullest extent in the next few years. They were to change not only the way people thought of nurses and nursing, but the way people thought of women.

As in all wars, many human beings were to die horrible and unnecessary deaths before it was over. Yet something good came out of the horror – a greater respect for the common soldier and wide reaching reforms in military organization and in the way all hospitals were run. Florence Nightingale was the key figure in these reforms.

She has gone down in history as The Lady With The Lamp, the nurse who walked among the wounded in the Crimean War.

The British Army was the best in the world. It could never be beaten: or so everyone in Britain believed in 1854. The soldiers in their bright uniforms marched to the ships that were to take them to the Crimean Peninsula on the Black Sea, banners shining in the sun, bands playing, little drummer boys proudly leading the parade.

This gallant army was to be defeated – not by another army, but by disease, lack of organization, cold and hunger.

In June, the British troops sailed north to help the Turks who were under siege. The area chosen for the campsite was a notorious breeding ground

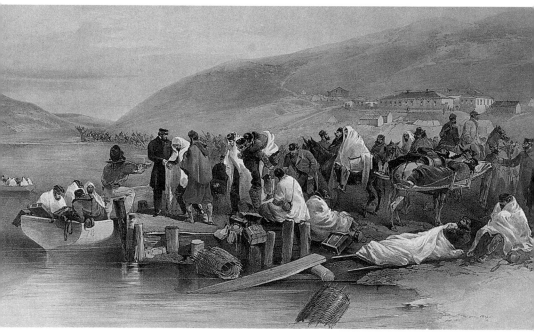

for cholera – an epidemic of the disease broke out almost immediately. All night the British soldiers could hear the splashing sound of corpses being tossed into the bay. Within three weeks, the army was rendered just about useless.

The British forces then turned their attention to the main objective of Sebastopol. Since there were not enough ships to take the army and its equipment across the Black Sea to the Crimean peninsula, the military leaders decided to transport only the troops. The pack animals, tents, cooking stoves, medical supplies, hospital marquees, bedding and stores were left behind.

Three days had been allowed for the transportation of troops across the Black Sea, but it took seventeen days. On board the ships there had been scarcely any food or water and cholera continued to run rife.

When the men landed in September they were ordered to leave their packs behind – they were simply too weak to carry them. The lack of supplies had already driven them to drink from the filthy puddles on the beaches. Men lay there, in the open, tortured with diarrhoea and dysentery.

Opposite top: The women say goodbye to soldiers dressed in their finery. The troops were over-confident as they set sail for the Crimean War. Within a week of arrival, and before the first battle had been fought, over one thousand men had died of disease.

The agony of victory

Thus the first battles in the Crimea were fought by men exhausted by disease and racked with thirst. Nevertheless this army of invalids had managed to cross the Alma, storm the heights above the river and force the Russian army to retreat into the city of Sebastopol. There were appalling casualties in this fighting.

They would have been better off killed outright. All the medical supplies were back at the campsite. There were no bandages, no splints, no anaesthetics of any kind to help the wounded. There were no candles or lamps; the surgeons worked by moonlight, while their patients lay on manure-covered straw in open ground.

Eventually the sick and wounded were packed into hospital ships to make the crossing back to Scutari. As many as 1500 men, weak and exhausted,

Opposite bottom: The British suffered disastrously in the first battles. Two thousand men were killed in the Battle of Inkerman alone. The wounded endured incredible hardships. They were taken on crude litters to the coast where they waited days for a ship to transport them to the hospital on the south coast of the Black Sea. Even if they survived the journey, many had wounds so badly infected that they would eventually die.

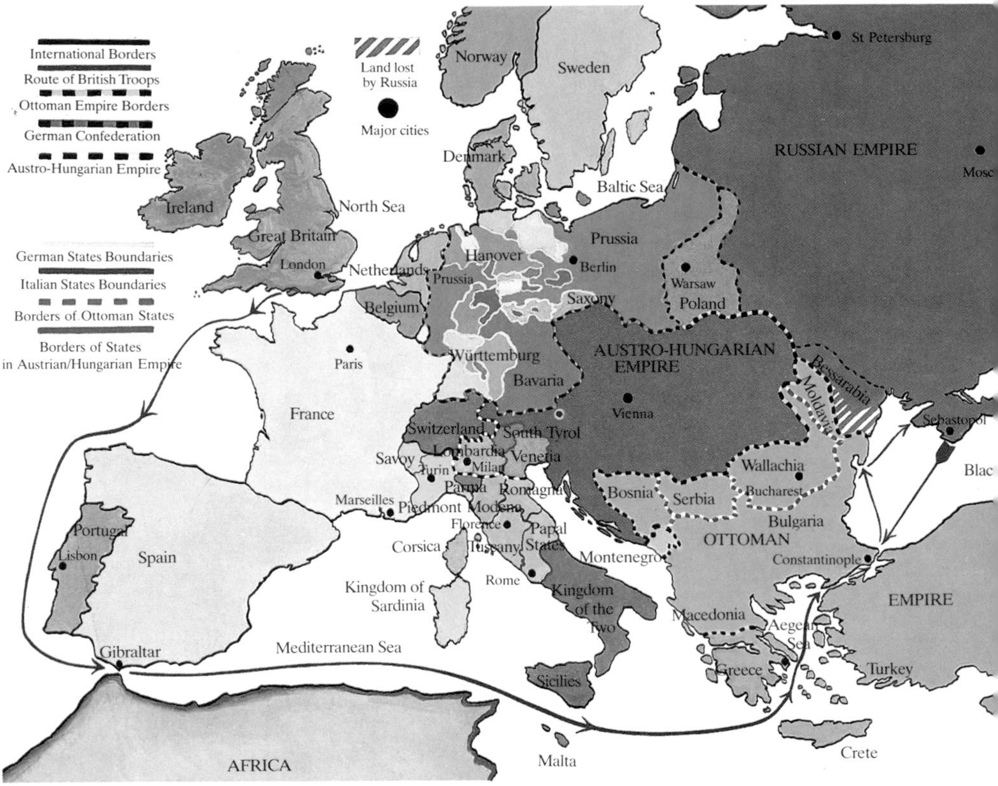
International Borders
Route of British Troops
Ottoman Empire Borders
German Confederation
Austro-Hungarian Empire
German States Boundaries
Italian States Boundaries
Borders of Ottoman States
Borders of States in Austrian/Hungarian Empire
Land lost by Russia
Major cities
Norway
Sweden
St Petersburg
RUSSIAN EMPIRE
Denmark
Baltic Sea
Ireland
North Sea
Great Britain
London
Netherlands
Hanover
Prussia
Berlin
Warsaw
Poland
Saxony
Belgium
Paris
Württemburg
Bavaria
AUSTRO-HUNGARIAN EMPIRE
Bessarabia
Moldavia
Vienna
France
Switzerland
South Tyrol
Sebastopol
Lombardia
Venetia
Savoy
Turin
Milan
Wallachia
Parma
Romagna
Bosnia
Serbia
Bucharest
Marseilles
Piedmont
Modena
Florence
Papal States
Bulgaria
OTTOMAN
Portugal
Lisbon
Spain
Corsica
Tuscany
Montenegro
Constantinople
Kingdom of Sardinia
Rome
Kingdom of the Two Sicilies
EMPIRE
Macedonia
Aegean Sea
Gibraltar
Mediterranean Sea
Greece
Turkey
Malta
Crete
AFRICA

Above: The route of the British fleet that sailed for Sebastopol in the Crimea. France, Turkey and Britain were allies against the Russians.

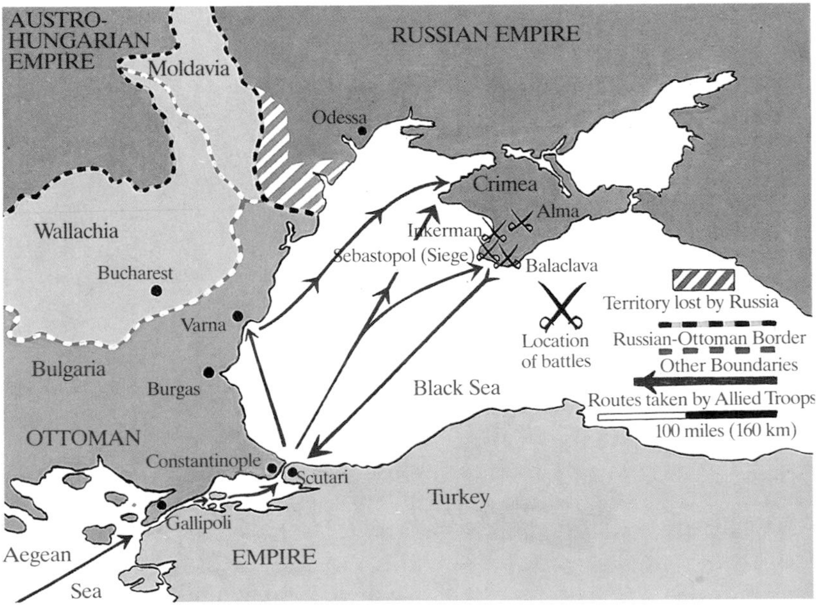
AUSTRO-HUNGARIAN EMPIRE
RUSSIAN EMPIRE
Moldavia
Odessa
Crimea
Alma
Wallachia
Inkerman
Sebastopol (Siege)
Balaclava
Bucharest
Territory lost by Russia
Varna
Location of battles
Russian-Ottoman Border
Other Boundaries
Bulgaria
Burgas
Black Sea
Routes taken by Allied Troops
100 miles (160 km)
OTTOMAN
Constantinople
Scutari
Turkey
Gallipoli
Aegean Sea
EMPIRE

Right: The main battles were fought at Balaclava, Inkerman and Sebastopol to the north of the Black Sea. The wounded were shipped over three hundred miles to the hospital at Scutari.

were crammed into one ship built to take only 250. But by the time the battle wounded began to arrive, the hospital was already full to overflowing. Before a single shot in the Crimean War had been fired, the cholera epidemic had thrown the Army's medical services into chaos.

The Barrack Hospital could provide no food because there was no kitchen. There were no beds, no linen, no cups to bring men parched with fever a sip of water. There were no tables or chairs. There were a few doctors but no operating tables. The Barrack Hospital was nothing but a skeleton of a building, full of men lying on the bare floors, half wrapped in blankets caked with blood and filth, crying out – if they still had the strength – for something to drink.

News from the front

To experienced military men this was nothing new. But to the rest of Great Britain this situation came as a great shock.

Something had to be done. And fast. The French had more surgeons and the Sisters of Charity to help in the field. The British had no one. Who could be sent to put things right, to nurse these suffering men?

To Sidney Herbert, Florence's old, faithful friend and now Secretary of War, there was only one answer – Florence herself. On October 15, Sidney Herbert sent a letter to Florence asking her to organize a body of nurses and to go out to Scutari as soon as possible.

Here was the work that Florence felt God had intended her to do. She knew, as Herbert knew, that it was a job only she could do.

Incredibly, even her family supported her: "It is a great and noble work," wrote sister Parthe. "One cannot but believe she was intended for it".

Florence accepted Herbert's proposal and, at the age of thirty-four, was appointed Superintendent of the Female Nursing Establishment of the English General Hospitals in Turkey. It was decided that forty nurses would go with her.

It was hard to find suitable nurses. But, somehow

"Then there was the question of Army hospitals though this was hardly a question. There were none. If a battlefield happened to be near a city, as was the field of Waterloo, civic hospitals were available but were far too small to cope with the enormous influx of the wounded and dying. Further, there were no Army nurses. There were orderlies, but many of them were pensioners so old and infirm they could scarce lift a stretcher."
Elizabeth Burton,
from "The Early Victorians at Home".

CARRYING THE FROST-BITTEN TO BALACLAVA.

Demoralized, frost-bitten troops are carried back to Balaclava. Many died on the way to hospital – often frozen upright in the saddle. Even when they got back to base, their chances were slim. Infection and inadequate food would kill thousands more.

or other, Florence got together a group of thirty-eight women – an ill-assorted party, but the best she could do. Some were professional nurses, some were nuns – the most efficient being five sisters from a Roman Catholic convent. On October 21, 1854 the party set out.

Florence arrives in Scutari

On November 5, 1854 Florence and her party entered the Barrack Hospital at Scutari.

Florence had been worried what to expect, but none of the descriptions had prepared her for the chaos and misery she found there. The bare corridors led to filthy wards. The central courtyard was a morass of stinking mud. There was rubbish and dirt everywhere. There were *four miles of beds* – if one could call them such. The wounded lay only a foot or so apart. It was a hotbed of infectious disease, and alive with vermin.

Florence had to tread carefully. All medical staff were firmly under the control of the military authorities. One false move and she might find herself, and her nurses, ordered home.

Organization had broken down. Everything required an application form, a permission slip, signed by two doctors. Valuable foodstuffs were lost or rotting because the correct applications had not been made – or because no one would accept authority to issue them. Any officials not applying in the correct way were in serious trouble and so they had become nervous about ordering *anything*.

The soldiers were regarded as "scum", "brutes", "blackguards" by the officers. Florence was warned not to "spoil" them. She found herself confronted by officers only interested in paper work and by Lord Stratford de Redclyffe Canning, the British Ambassador to Constantinople. He had tremendous influence but he lived in luxury in a palace and simply ignored the misery and pain and filth that the soldiers endured.

Rules and regulations

There was nothing at the Barrack Hospital. No operating tables. No medical supplies. No furniture. Rats and fleas infested the nurses' rooms – and there were no lamps or candles. At night they lay in darkness listening to the scampering of rats' feet.

The doctors resented Florence and ignored her. She knew she must win the trust of the doctors before she could do anything. She gave her nurses careful instructions. Despite the anguish of having to leave the wounded, they *must* wait until they were officially asked to help.

A huge new consignment of men, terribly wounded at the battle of Balaclava, arrived on November 6. Still Florence held her nurses in check. They found what linen they could and made bandages, stump rests, pillows, shirts. And waited.

Even if she was asked to do something, Florence forced herself to accept the regulations. Only in the kitchen could she get any foothold. What she found there disgusted her. There were no saucepans or kettles. Tea was made in coppers in which meat had just been boiled.

Florence set to work. She had brought wine, beef essence and portable stoves with her. She stuck

The Scutari Barrack Hospital before the twenty thousand wounded men arrived. Scutari was literally a barracks, not a hospital. There were four miles of long, dirty halls which would become four miles of crowded beds. There were rats, leaking roofs and no running water. The lavatories were blocked and overflowed into the wards. Florence arrived with forty nurses – only twelve would survive.

"Roll Call", the famous painting by Lady Butler, wife of a serving officer, who portrayed the suffering and courage of ordinary men caught up in war. This picture shows the count of the survivors after the Battle of Balaclava.

Opposite: The blinded, crippled and wounded struggle back from the front, helping their friends as best they can. Their lives will now depend on good food and good, clean conditions in hospital – which Florence Nightingale was fighting against all odds to provide.

strictly to every rule, so no one could object to her actions. Nothing was given to a patient without a signed slip from a doctor, but gradually the poor, sick, hungry men were eating food that did them good instead of making them even more ill.

No one knows how long this situation might have continued – but on November 9 a great tide of sick and wounded swept down upon Scutari. The doctors and officials were forced to acknowledge Florence's existence and to accept her help and that of her nurses.

The great task begins

The British suffered a defeat at the Battle of Balaclava. The nearby camp was soon a quagmire of filth – and bodies and the amputated limbs of the wounded floated in the tideless sea. The place stank and cholera raged through the army.

The Battle of Inkermann followed. Although it was a British victory, it only added to the wounded.

When they read of the suffering, the people of Britain had donated shiploads of sheets, bandages and food. The problem was that the incompetent medical officers would not release them. Many of the soldiers called Florence Nightingale "The Lady with the Hammer". She actually broke into the supply stores to relieve the desperate patients.

Winter was setting in. Men grubbed in the frozen ground with bleeding hands to find a few dead roots to burn. There was nowhere to cook a hot meal. There was nowhere to sleep but frozen mud. The only track down was impassable.

Disease, gangrene – it seemed hell on earth: and a flood of victims were sent to swell the huge numbers already at Scutari.

Florence had to admire the military medical staff. They were on their feet for twenty-four hours at a time, but still they could not make any real impression on the constant influx of patients. Men were jammed in to every space, lying on bare boards with their heads on their boots for want of a pillow. Florence estimated that at least one thousand men were suffering from dysentery. There were twenty chamber pots. These were emptied into vast vats – but the orderlies dodged the awful job of emptying them and they were sometimes left for twenty-four hours on end.

As if this misery was not enough, on November 14 a tremendous storm broke – and carried away whatever tents the army had erected, leaving the men without cover of any kind. Every single ship was sunk, including one newly arrived with a cargo of desperately needed warm clothes and stores.

Florence takes over

By November 30, the hospital administration had broken down. Now the officials simply had to acknowledge Florence's presence – for she had private donations from charities in Britain and she had the ability to get the essential supplies.

She took over very quietly, determined to avoid confrontation if she could. At last, no one was allowed to dodge any necessary job, however loathesome.

There had been no washing of linen – and every shirt was crawling with vermin. Florence ordered boilers – and boilers were installed. The chamber pots and vats were emptied and cleaned. As in Harley Street, Florence gave great attention to detail. She made an inventory of every single item

An idealized picture, but painted to show the concern Florence had for each man. She made sure that after the horrors of battle, they were bathed, their wounds dressed and that clean clothes and a good meal were given to each man.

Many of the troops were disembarked at Varna in Bulgaria. The camp was on a site notorious for cholera and over one thousand cases were sent back to Scutari.

"The Thin Red Line", the 93rd Highlanders at Balaclava, painted by Caton Woodville. During the war, Britain and France lost between them eighty-two thousand soldiers in battle. Disease and the terrible Crimean winter killed far more than sword or gunfire.

"Her calmness, her resource, her power to take action raised her to the position of a goddess. The men adored her.... The doctors came to be absolutely dependent on her...."

Cecil Woodham Smith, from "Florence Nightingale".

that was needed and got them – trays, tables, clocks, towels, soap, cups, plates and cutlery.

At the beginning of December Lord Raglan had warned that he was sending five hundred more wounded and sick to the already over-crowded hospital and Florence needed space desperately. One wing of the hospital had been badly damaged by fire and left to fall into near-ruin. Florence pressed to have the wing put into good order. After endless difficulties with Lord Stratford and the Turkish workmen employed to do the repairs, she took it upon herself to get the work done, paying for it out of her own money and donated funds.

Everything that should have come through army supplies now came through Miss Nightingale. The army officials were incensed – but Florence ignored them and went doggedly on.

"Unparalleled calamity"

The winter campaign was horror upon horror. In the January of 1855, the plight of the wounded became appalling. It was, Florence wrote, "calamity unparalleled in the history of calamity". The numbers of patients multiplied to a most terrifying degree. In that January there were twelve thousand men in hospital. Florence was fighting most terrible odds. And yet still she brought her mind to bear on what should be done. She wrote out systematic, carefully reasoned plans for the intelligent reorganization of the hospitals. She dealt with both the present and the future.

One of the greatest anxieties was the ever-rising number of deaths at the Barrack Hospital, despite the improvements that had been made. Men were more likely to die at the Barrack Hospital than if they remained at the crude, freezing, regimental hospitals on the heights outside Sebastopol. Whatever was done, the numbers kept on going up. At the end of December an epidemic broke out. Four surgeons, three nurses and hundreds of soldiers died in three weeks.

The news of this appalling state of affairs was published in the British newspapers and people began to demand that the whole tragedy of the Crimea be investigated. The wave of indignation forced the government to send out a Sanitary Commission at the end of February 1855.

Reform at the Barrack Hospital

The Commission inspected the Barrack Hospital from top to bottom. No wonder the death rate was so high. The entire building was standing on a network of badly decaying sewers – the whole structure was soaked through with decay and filth and disease. Every movement of the air had carried death through the crowded wards. In addition, the water supply was infected.

In the first two weeks of cleaning out this horror, 556 handcarts of refuse were removed, and 24 assorted dead animals and 2 dead horses were buried.

Conditions at the hospital improved, but terrible mistakes were still being made, through bungling and lack of real organization. One instance was when a transport ship was being loaded with several hundred wounded soldiers. It took from mid-November until early December. For two weeks, the men lay on the bare decks with nothing to protect them from the winter weather. The man responsible, Dr. Lawson, was later reprimanded, only to be appointed Senior Medical Officer at the Barrack Hospital. It shocked Florence how often officials who had opposed every reform and blocked her work at every turn were often the most noted, particularly after the war.

The lady with the lamp

By the spring of 1855 Florence was exhausted. At times she was on her knees for eight hours at a stretch, dressing wounds. She had none of the drugs or dressings of a modern hospital ward – she had to make do with what she had.

The thing that kept her going was the incredible bravery of the men. They tried never to complain, never to betray their agony, fear and homesickness. If Florence had in the past gained a reputation for

Once the situation at Scutari was under control, Florence Nightingale visited the medical stations in the battle areas. She rode out in all weathers – and paid the price by becoming desperately ill.

Florence Nightingale became famous as "The Lady with the Lamp", and became a legend in her own time. The wounded loved to see her, because she so obviously cared what was happening, and fought for better conditions for them. They had seen terrible things in battle and this gently-spoken woman was a reminder that there was still sanity and kindness in the world.

coldness, no one, save stubborn officials, saw it now. The men always remembered her patience, her kindness – even her fun. She stood by them when they were forced to endure surgery. She gave them new hope just by moving among them on her rounds, speaking to one, smiling at another.

If she couldn't see them during the day she made her rounds at night, lighting her way along the four miles of beds with a Turkish lamp. One soldier wrote home that the men kissed her shadow on the wall as she passed.

In turn, Florence's respect for them would in years to come change forever the European attitude to "the common soldiery". Long after Scutari, Florence Nightingale would still be fighting to improve their lot.

Crimean Fever

Florence worked on at everything that came to hand and once the Barrack Hospital was in a satisfactory condition, she decided it was time to go to the Crimean hospitals. But, at last, she paid the penalty. Her strength failed her while she was inspecting conditions at Balaclava and she was forced to take to her bed with the Crimean Fever. For two weeks she lay at the very edge of death, but even when she was delirious, she wrote and wrote and wrote – lists, orders, recommendations.

When she was able to leave her room at last people were shocked at the change in her. She was pale and terribly thin, her nose prominent in her drawn face. She would never again be as strong and vigorous as she once had been.

Trouble met her as she went back to work. The army, the nurses and the nuns all seemed to be having their own private war and the weight of it came squarely on poor Florence.

Her family decided that someone must go to Scutari to be with Florence. Aunt Mai volunteered and on September 16, 1855, she and an experienced store clerk arrived there. Aunt Mai was horrified by Flo's frailty and pallor – and by the bitter feuds and pettiness by which she was surrounded. She set to, helping with the office work. She wrote of Florence, "She has attained a most wonderful calm. No irritation of temper, no hurry or confusion of manner ever appears for a moment. Food, rest, temperature never interfere with her work".

"What a comfort it was to see her pass even. She would speak to one, and nod and smile to as many more; but she could not do it all you know. We lay there by hundreds; but we could kiss her shadow as it fell and lay our heads on the pillow again content."
A soldier in the Barrack Hospital.

The Nightingale Fund

In England, Florence was seen as the light of the Crimea. The country was bursting with Nightingale souvenirs – mugs and plates, pottery busts, poems, wildly inaccurate biographies.

A racehorse was named after her, as was a lifeboat. Florence, level-headed as ever, was totally unmoved. She had lived with the stark reality, and she knew how much still needed to be done.

Money was subscribed to make a presentation – "something of the teapot and bracelet variety" Parthe wrote, wryly. But so much money was received that it was decided to set up a Nightingale Fund to help establish an institute for the training

"What the horrors of war are no one can imagine. They are not wounds and blood, and fever, spotted and low, and dysentery, chronic and acute, and cold and heat and famine. They are intoxication, drunken brutality, demoralization and disorder on the part of the inferior; jealousies, meanness, indifference, selfish brutality on the part of the superior."
Florence Nightingale.

The remains of an army go home. They had marched to the troop ships with bands playing and flags flying. They had won their battles – but had been defeated by dirt, disease and bad organization. Florence had saved many, but her pioneering work was to ensure that thousands more in the years to come were given the care they deserved.

"No one can feel for the army as I do. People must have seen that long dreadful winter to know what it was. I can never forget."

Florence Nightingale.

---

of nurses. It was suggested that the soldiers contribute a day's pay to the Fund. The troops subscribed nearly £9,000 (Over £200,000 in today's money.)

Florence's mother, Fanny, was overcome with emotion. She wrote to tell Flo how proud she was of her. Florence, setting aside the past, wrote back, "My reputation has not been a boon in my work; but if you have been pleased that is enough."

Battle of words

In December, The Chief of Medical Staff, Dr. Hall, had forwarded a report by the Chief Purveyor, that accused Florence of insubordination and her nurses of dishonesty, extravagance, disobedience, inefficiency and immorality. It was a pack of lies and Florence was appalled.

A tremendous battle of words, letters, and meetings broke out between the government and the people trying to blacken Florence's name.

But at the beginning of 1856 a Commission into the Supply of the British Army in the Crimea put its report before Parliament. It confirmed all that Florence had reported. Incredibly, though, Dr. John Hall was awarded the Knight Commander of the Bath, K.C.B. "Knight of the Crimean Burial grounds, I suppose," wrote Florence bitterly. "I am in a state of chronic rage. I who saw the men come down through all that long, long dreadful winter without other covering than a dirty blanket and a pair of old regimental trousers, when we knew the stores were bursting with warm clothing, living skeletons devoured by vermin, ulcerated, hopeless, speechless, dying like the Greeks as they wrapped their heads in their blankets and spoke never a word.... Can we hear of the promotion of the men who caused this colossal calamity, we who saw it?"

The government triumphed and on March 16, 1856 a despatch was published stating Florence's position. It read, "Miss Nightingale is recognised by Her Majesty's Government as General Superintendent of the Female Nursing Establishment of the military hospitals of the Army."

Her word was to be law. All her enemies were defeated at one blow.

"Two figures emerged from the Crimea as heroic, the soldier and the nurse. In each case a transformation in public estimation took place, and in each case the transformation was due to Miss Nightingale."
Cecil Woodham Smith, from "Florence Nightingale".

Return to England

Florence was exhausted but triumphant. And soon after, on April 29, 1856, peace was declared. The fighting was at an end, but the threat of disease was not. It was essential to get the men home before the summer came with the heat that bred cholera. On July 16, 1856 the last patient left the Barrack Hospital. Florence's work was over.

On July 28 she and Aunt Mai sailed for France. Florence left Aunt Mai in Paris and secretly continued on to England alone. She wanted to avoid the crowds and the grand receptions that had been planned for her return. On the morning after her arrival, she went to the convent of the Bermondsey nuns and spent the morning there in prayer and quietness. In the afternoon she went quietly to the family's country home.

But if the war was over, if awards were heaped on her, Florence could not forget. The capable, efficient organizer, apparently unbreakable in her

Florence fever swept the country!! Sentimental souvenirs of every description were produced.

resolve, wrote in her private diary:

"Oh my poor men, I am a bad mother to come home and leave you in your Crimean graves – 73% in eight regiments in six months from disease alone – who thinks of that now?"

Florence, the heroine

Florence was exhausted, the life drained out of her by her struggles in the Crimea. She was only thirty-six, but she felt her work must surely be over – now she could rest, recover, have a little time to herself. Florence Nightingale did not realize that the main work of her life was only just beginning. She had nearly forty years of active working life ahead of her.

During the first months after the war, she was drowning in congratulatory letters, in proposals of marriage, in hysterical admiration. She hated being a celebrity and what she called the "fuz-buz about my name". So she signed no autographs, granted no interviews, wrote no letters to her admirers, attended no public functions. After a while people stopped expecting her to react to the "fuz-buz" and life quietened down.

The Victorians created a sentimental image of Florence Nightingale. She was the "lady with the lamp" – a kind, gentle, soft-hearted woman who bent over the beds of sick and dying men to offer comfort and hope. But that was only one side of Florence's character. She was also a strong-willed, diplomatic and extremely intelligent woman. When the "lady with the lamp" took up a cause, she was a force to be reckoned with.

The Crimean War revealed causes aplenty to Florence. She already knew that nurses needed to be properly trained. But her experiences with the staff at Scutari convinced her more than ever that she must find a way to make nursing a respectable profession, with standards of conduct and achievement that all nurses would have to measure up to. She knew that hospitals had to be changed too – many of the deaths at Scutari were caused by the conditions at the hospital and nothing else. Florence had spent years studying hospitals all over Europe – no one knew more about what went on in them or what action must be taken for their reform. In the years to come she would tackle these problems and many others, from the administration of the workhouses in Liverpool to the health and living conditions of the entire country of India. But first she wanted to change the British Army.

The memories of Scutari and Balaclava haunted her, but all that suffering had taught the army medical authorities nothing. The system continued in every army barrack and hospital, the system that had been at the root of the chaos and misery of the Crimea. Florence could not ignore it.

Queen Victoria helps

And then a wonderful opportunity came. The Queen and Prince Albert wanted to hear her story from her own lips. She set to work to prepare evidence that would convince them of the need for army reform. She visited military hospitals and

Below: Victorian romantic sentiments clouded the real achievements of Florence Nightingale. Note the picture on the left, with Florence walking moonlit wards clutching an armful of roses! The incompetent officers who had faced the tough, determined and uncompromising nurse in the Crimea did not remember this side of Florence Nightingale.

NOTES ON NVRSING

Queen Victoria had a deep admiration for Florence Nightingale's achievements in the Crimean War. She presented Florence with this brooch, inscribed "Blessed are the Merciful". The Queen gave invaluable backing to Florence in her campaign for reform of the army health service.

barracks to inspect conditions, often for over twelve hours a day. When she arrived home she would start writing again. Sometimes now, and for the next three decades, she would work for twenty-two hours at a time.

In September, just two months afer her return from the Crimea, she went to Balmoral in Scotland for a meeting with the Queen and Prince Albert. They were delighted with her and listened carefully to everything she put before them.

"I wish we had her at the War Office", the Queen wrote to her Commander in Chief.

They asked her back again and again.

It was a real beginning, but Florence now had to win over the chief government ministers. As an outsider she could not change basic methods in the army without being an important politician. And as a woman, she could not be a politician. The only way open to her was to work through some of the leading men of the time. This, she achieved. Sidney Herbert and at least four other top men devoted all their spare time to her causes. They respected her as *the* expert in hospital conditions. And her modest, methodical manner meant they enjoyed working for her.

The negotiations brought six months more of tiring hospital visits, persuasion and writing – reducing Florence to a shadow.

Army reform

At last in May 1857 a Commission to study the whole question of the army medical service began to sit. The price was high. Florence was doing this gruelling work because it was vital, not because she had chosen it. She had changed. Now she was more brilliant in argument than ever, more efficient, more knowledgeable, more persistent and penetrating in her reasoning, scrupulously just, mathematically accurate – but she was pushing herself to the very limits of her capacity at the expense of all joy.

That summer of 1857 was a nightmare for Florence – not only was she working day and night to instruct the politicians sitting on the Commission, she was writing her own confidential report about her experiences. All this while Parthe and Mama lay about on sofas, telling each other not to get exhausted arranging flowers.

It took Florence only six months to complete her own one-thousand-page Confidential Report, *Notes on Matters affecting the Health, Efficiency and Hospital Administration of the British Army.* It was an incredibly clear, deeply-considered volume. Every single thing she had learned from the Crimea was there – every statement she made was backed by hard evidence.

Florence Nightingale was basically arguing for prevention rather than cure. It was a new idea then and many politicians and army medical men felt it was revolutionary and positively cranky. They grimly opposed Florence and her allies.

She was forced to prove that the soldiers were dying because of their basic living conditions. She

Below: The Commission (all men) set up in 1857 to study the army medical service. Several of the members not only deeply admired Florence Nightingale, but took instruction directly from her. Her criticisms of the army were merciless.

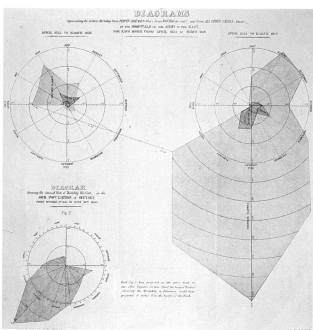

Above left: A cartoon of the day, showing how army recruits were seen by the press – as drunken, lazy oafs. Florence saw them differently – as ordinary people, driven by poverty into the army and treated abominably.

Above right: This diagram shows Florence's detailed way of presenting her research. She was able to demonstrate that for every soldier killed in battle in the Crimean War, seven died of infections and preventable disease. Florence became the pioneer of preventative medicine. Better food, cleanliness and good ventilation could prevent disease and death, and she proved this by painstaking research.

had inspected dozens of hospitals and barracks and now exposed them as damp, filthy and unventilated, with dirty drains and infected water supplies. She showed that the soldiers' diet was poor. She collected statistics which proved that the death rate for young soldiers *in peace time* was double that of the normal population.

She showed that, though the army took only the fittest young men, every year 1,500 were killed by neglect, poor food and disease. She declared "Our soldiers enlist to death in the barracks", and this became the battle cry of her supporters.

The public, too, was on her side. The more the anti-reformers dragged their feet, the greater the reform pressure became.

Florence did not win an outright victory against her opponents, but many changes came through. Soon some barracks were rebuilt and within three years the death rate would halve.

The intense work on the Commission was now over, but Florence was to continue studying, planning and pressing for army medical reform for the next thirty years.

Collapse

On August 11 she collapsed completely – she had not been alone for four years and she longed for silence. She was living on tea. She was so ill someone actually wrote her obituary and one newspaper got ready to publish it the moment she died.

Yet there was still so much to do. She *could* not die. She hadn't the time.

Instead she retreated. When Florence returned to London Aunt Mai came with her. Aunt Mai had stood by Florence in rough times before, had even gone out to work with her in the Crimea. Now with her help Florence was finally able to turn the tables on her sister and mother. Every time they threatened to visit she had an "attack" and Aunt Mai wrote pleading letters, saying that Florence's life "hung by a thread", that they must stay away. And stay away they finally did.

A proposal for Parthe

Florence's attempt to keep her family at a distance was aided by a man called Sir Harry Verney. After paying a series of calls on her in the summer of 1857, he had proposed marriage. Florence, needless to say, had turned him down.

Sir Harry transferred his affections to Florence's older sister, Parthe, and in 1858 their engagement was announced. Fanny and Parthe occupied themselves with wedding preparations.

Shortly after the wedding Florence moved into the annexe of the Burlington Hotel. It was spacious and quiet. Florence no longer saw friends, went to parties or to concerts. Aunt Mai looked after her. Florence made plans for her own funeral, but from a semi-reclining position on her sofa managed to work harder than she'd ever worked before.

People now began to demand that she apply her knowledge to *civilian* hospitals, which she found to be "just as bad or worse" than military hospitals. In 1859 she published a book called *Notes on Hospitals*. It showed the world why people feared to be taken into hospitals and how matters could be remedied.

"Her Notes on Hospitals (1859) revolutionised the theory of hospital construction and hospital management. She was immediately recognised as the leading expert upon all the questions involved, her advice flowed unceasingly, so that there is no great hospital body which does not bear upon it the impress of her mind."
Lythan Strachey,
from "Eminent Victorians".

A benign Florence Nightingale with some of her nurses. One of the secrets of her success was that she was a perfectionist. She had seen the results of sloppy planning in the Crimea and for the rest of her life she fought for high standards. No detail was too small. She had an opinion on everything, from the width of operating room doors to the shade of the paint. Somehow she passed her passion for caring and perfectionism on to others. And she never lost her kindness – a nurse taking up a new post would find a note and flowers in her room from Miss Nightingale.

Florence set forth the then revolutionary theory that simply by improving the construction and physical maintenance, hospital deaths could be greatly reduced. More windows, better ventilation, improved drainage, less cramped conditions, and regular scrubbing of the floors, walls and bed frames were basic measures that every hospital could take.

Florence soon became an expert on the building of hospitals and all over the world hospitals were established according to her specifications. She wrote hundreds and hundreds of letters from her sofa in London inquiring about sinks and saucepans, locks and laundry rooms. No detail was too small for her considered attention. She worked out ideas for the most efficient way to distribute clean linen, the best method of keeping food hot, the correct number of inches between beds. She intended to change the administration of hospitals from top to toe. Lives depended upon detail.

Florence Nightingale succeeded. All over the world Nightingale-style hospitals would be built. And Florence would continue to advise on hospital plans for over forty years. Today's hospitals with

their flowers and bright, clean and cheerful wards are a direct result of her work.

"Notes on Nursing"

One of the hospitals she advised was St. Thomas's in London. As she consulted with them about their plans to build a new hospital, she decided it would be a good place to establish a school for nurses.

While the negotiations went forward she wrote a small book about nursing to be used by ordinary women. Published in 1859, just four years after the Crimea, *Notes on Nursing: What It Is and What It Is Not* was an instant success. Sidney Herbert wrote that it was "more interesting than a novel"; a writer described her daughter and a friend paying a round of visits and finding a copy on every table.

Like all Florence's work, *Notes* was revolutionary, although it contained nothing that isn't accepted today as basic good hygiene.

Florence also described with great sensitivity the suffering, both physical and mental, of a sick person, and attacked the conventional notion of a nurse. "It seems a commonly received idea among men, and even among women themselves," she wrote, "that it requires nothing but a disappointment in love, or incapacity in other things, to turn a woman into a good nurse."

The Nightingale nurses

To put this idea to rights, Florence needed to present the world with a different sort of nurse. Many doctors of the time were against all professional nursing training. They felt enough could be learned by experience and simple instruction on the spot. Women were still regarded as the weaker and more stupid sex – even with the example of Florence before men's eyes. But six months after publishing the *Notes* she was able, with the £45,000 from the Nightingale Fund, to set up a Training School for Nurses, attached to St. Thomas's Hospital.

Nightingale nurses were to be trained to train others, and to take posts where they could establish

"A nurse returning to the north found a luncheon-basket waiting in her railway carriage; another, who had been ill, received a diet sheet with the note: 'Get the things out of my money.' Run-down nurses were invited to convalesce for a weekend in bed. Each probationer was invited, by herself, to tea, and given a present, often a cake. One of the young women, dressed in her best to obey the summons, heard at the last moment that the poverty of the guest's attire determined the size of the cake. Hastily changing into her oldest clothes, she returned from the tea-party with a cake large enough to feed all thirty-six probationers."

Elspeth Huxley,
from "Florence Nightingale"

the high standards that Florence had outlined.

Every candidate was hand picked and had to have a character reference. They were issued with neat, sensible uniforms. Discipline was strict, but those accepted were to have rooms to themselves and Florence sent flowers, books, maps and pictures to make the school a pleasant place in which to live and work. No nurse had ever before been given the chance to study in this way.

Within a few months requests for Nightingale nurses were flooding in – the Nightingale Training School was succeeding. Soon its reputation was to spread worldwide. Within fifteen years, hospitals all over the world were asking for Nightingale nurses to start new schools. In 1867 a group was sent to Sydney, Australia, and by the early 1880s nurses at most of the big hospitals in the British Isles, Canada, Germany, Sweden and the United States had been trained at the School.

Once nurses were seen as heavy drinkers with loose sexual morals. Today nursing has become one of the most respected professions in the world. That change is largely due to Florence Nightingale and her single-minded determination.

Today, nurses are highly qualified and respected. Their public image is a world away from the drunken layabouts they were seen as when Florence Nightingale started out. She is recognized across the world as the pioneer of modern nursing.

A time of loss

In 1860, Florence was to find herself more and more alone. First, a colleague who was drafting the new Army Medical Regulations died suddenly. Then Aunt Mai returned to her own family. Finally, Sidney Herbert became so ill he was forced to resign from the War Office. Blinded by her yearning for further progress, she could not forgive him. She felt he had betrayed her.

Two months later Sidney Herbert died. His last words were "Poor Florence ... poor Florence ... our joint work unfinished".

Florence was horrified to hear the news. He had endured so much of her anger and reproach, he had worked so unceasingly for her causes. "And his angelic temper with me I shall never forget."

Herbert's death was a serious loss to Florence, not only because he was a great and dear friend, but because he was her door to the War Office. She had always worked with and through him. Without him, she was shut out – his death meant that the cause of Army Reform came to a halt. Florence, as she recovered from her grief, knew she would have to direct her vast knowledge and passion for change elsewhere.

In 1861 the American Civil War had broken out and Florence was asked for urgent help in case Britain became involved.

In order to get it all organized on time, Florence had to work day and night and, inevitably, collapsed again. She was not expected to live, but by January 1862 she could sit up in bed. But she could not walk and was not to leave her room for six years.

There was a constant stream of important visitors. Politicians, hospital administrators, all called on her to take advice or instruction. She conducted her vital business from her sofa – usually she was surrounded by at least three cats! She never lost her eye for detail. She never rested and would write letters, books and reports into the small hours.

For the remaining fifty years of her life Florence Nightingale would be handicapped and unable to walk. When she overworked or when she became

"Her position was extraordinary. She was, as the men round her delighted to call her, the Commander-in-Chief. She collected the facts, she collated and verified them, she drew the conclusions, she put the conclusions down on paper and finally, she taught them to the men who were her mouthpiece."
Cecil Woodham Smith, from "Florence Nightingale".

upset (usually because of her family!) her condition would worsen. We do not know exactly what was wrong but she suffered from weakness, fatigue and breathlessness.

She refused to see visitors unless they were connected with her work. "Flo's solitary confinement system" was how one friend described her way of life. The friend used the word "system" because from now on Florence made the decision to live her secluded, bedridden life on purpose – she knew it was the only way she could have the time and strength to continue working on her task.

More work than ever

And work she did. Although she seldom saw them personally, she received a constant flow of papers from various government officials. If a minister needed expert advice he contacted Miss Nightingale. If a government official needed a sanitary regulation drafted he sent it along to Florence. He knew he would get it back quickly and in a form he could use right away. By now she was an expert not only on questions of health and hospitals, but on government legislation and departments as well.

From the quiet and comfort of her bedroom, she drew up warrants and regulations, drafted minutes, wrote memoranda and letters, and of course, composed instructions. Such was her genius for administration that some of her innovations stayed in use long after her death. In 1947, an investigating committee commented on how well the cost-accounting system of the Army Medical Services worked when much newer methods had failed and had to be discontinued. They asked who had thought up the system. Florence Nightingale, came the answer.

Florence, at forty-two, was convinced that she had only a short time to live. However, she would survive till the age of ninety and for at least thirty of these years she would be one of the most powerful people in the country. Her campaigns for reform would continue, demanding improvements in the living conditions of soldiers, in hospital buildings

Opposite: Florence grown plump and peaceful, the days of "The Lady with the Lamp" far in the past – but still working for nursing, for the army, for the poor. She was infinitely kind to her nurses, showing them the same concern she had once given to the desperately sick governesses she had tended in her youth and to the dying soldiers she had held in the Crimean War.

The conditions in workhouses were so terrible that people would starve and go without seeing a doctor rather than enter a workhouse.

and in nurses training. She would achieve world-changing reforms, with no official position or secretarial help – lying on her sofa!

The army in India

Now, however, it was demanded that she turn her attention to India. This project would occupy her for more than thirty years. The health of the British army in the sub-continent, then a huge and vital part of the British Empire, must be improved. Statistics revealed that for years the death rate in the army in India had been sixty-nine per thousand – deaths caused not by the heat, but by lack of drainage and bad water. The soldiers washed in pie dishes. The barracks were crammed with men. Hospital diseases were rampant.

The Indian troops were even worse off. The poor men had no rations, no barracks, no toilets, no washing facilities, no kitchens – nothing. The native people, too, lived in utter squalor.

Florence realized that it was a matter of improving the health of the *whole of India.* It was a daunting task. Confined to her bed, she prepared another massive two-thousand-page report, as brilliant as those that had gone before.

But delay followed delay. 1864 drifted into 1865 and nothing had really been done in India.

Florence was, again, in despair. She could not move without help and yet she felt deeply committed to fighting on for her causes. Her nerves were in an appalling state. She could not bear anyone in the room, nor any movement nor sound.

After thirteen months shut in her room preparing yet another report on the Indian question, Flo at last accomplished something – a Sanitary Department in the India Office was to be set up and Annual Reports were to be submitted from now on.

Meanwhile Florence worked on other projects. She was still deeply involved in the reorganization of nursing, the Poor Laws, hospital reform, childbirth and nurses training. Her work load was gigantic and she was more than ever well respected and influential. She was forty-seven.

Workhouse reform

And now came the question of workhouses. In December 1864 a pauper had died in London's Holborn workhouse – from "filthiness caused by gross neglect". Florence was heard to thank God for the poor fellow's death, for it gave her a stick with which to beat the Poor Law Board.

In Britain, the threat of being sent to the workhouse was a nightmare that hung over the lives of the very poor. The Victorians reasoned that if such places were dreadful enough, people would struggle even harder not to be sent there. But bad harvests, illness, family tragedies and old age sent the poor to these institutions, however grim they were. Husbands were parted from wives and the inmates were made to feel degraded and a burden on society. The conditions were often horrific.

In 1865, Nightingale Nurses were eventually allowed into the Liverpool workhouse infirmary on

Workhouses were for all the most destitute people. The disabled, insane, orphans and the sick poor were all kept there – in dreadful filthy conditions. Florence spent years campaigning for reform of these conditions and for the training of nurses to help in workhouses.

Fildes' great picture of the desperate poor waiting for admission to the charity wards. The notices on the wall are the artist's comment on what crimes these sad, hungry, frozen people would be driven to. Florence was deeply concerned with the reform of workhouses.

an experimental basis. For the first time, nursing of the poor was to be done by trained staff. The results were encouraging and Florence pressed for an Act of Parliament so that wide-ranging workhouse reform could be made.

In 1867, when the Metropolitan Poor Act was eventually passed, she wrote, "We have obtained some things, the removal of two thousand lunatics, eighty fever and smallpox cases and all the remaining children out of the workhouses" – besides other reforms. "This is a beginning, we shall get more in time." She drove herself harder than ever before.

Back to St. Thomas's

Following an investigation into falling standards at the Nightingale Training School, Florence, in the spring of 1872, realized that reform and reorganization were needed. She decided to live nearer to the hospital and to devote her life to the school and the hospital.

Her plans fell through when she had to concentrate on looking after her parents. She divided her time during the next three years between caring for them and her work on the reorganization of the Nightingale school.

On January 10, 1874 her father fell downstairs and died.

Now the burden of having to deal with all the family's problems and the full responsibility of her mother overwhelmed her. Grief-stricken for her father she wrote: "My life seems utter shipwreck".

During the next quiet years she worked on steadily. She kept control of the Nightingale School, and the progress and successes of her nurses were a great and constant joy. She delighted in the letters that came to her from all over the world. She had achieved so much. The role of women was forever changed. Attitudes to the ordinary soldier had been transformed. Childbirth, hospital building, the treatment of poor people – all these major reforms were due to Florence Nightingale. And she was still totally involved, supporting new reforms and improvements.

Failure in India

But in one field she felt she had failed. It was India. After another four years of detailed work, she wrote in her diary, "Oh that I could do something for India!"

In her biography, Cecil Woodham Smith says that by 1879, "She [Florence] had reached a depth of despair: progress in India was at a standstill; out of the effort and sacrifice of twenty years nothing had been achieved."

Yet, she had written to every medical officer in India and had compiled a detailed study of their reports. Simply through better hygiene and clean water supplies, army deaths had fallen dramatically. But Florence felt the suffering and poverty of the ordinary people as a weight on her life.

In June that year her chief supporter, the Viceroy of India, died and the proposed work was shelved. No commission on irrigation had been set up; sanitary works recommended over fifteen years ago had not been started. Reform had failed.

Then, on February 2, 1880 her mother, Fanny,

Opposite top: Florence Nightingale in old age, a serene and beautiful old lady. She combined in her personality the best of two qualities – firmness and kindness. She had always been loved, almost worshipped. Many leading politicians and young nurses literally gave their lives to Florence Nightingale and her causes.

Bottom left: The bedroom where Florence Nightingale spent the last years of her life. She died here when she was ninety.

Botttom right: Claydon House, where Florence Nightingale spent her last years. She came from a world of comfort and dignity and need never have so much as noticed the poor and the suffering, but stayed cocooned in her wealthy world.

died. Florence, at sixty, was truly free at last.

She had written in 1879, "Do you know what have been the hardest years of my life? Not the Crimean War. Not the five years with Sidney Herbert at the War Office when I sometimes worked twenty-two hours a day, but the last five years and three quarters since my father's death."

Somehow, though, those terrible years had healed all the old bitterness. Nursing poor Fanny and getting to know Parthe better had given Florence a quietness and acceptance. Now she was far more gentle and forgiving. The family turned to her whenever they needed reassurance and advice. Even her defeats now seemed no longer to trouble her the way they once had.

She devoted decades to her causes.

Despite her often recurring sense of failure, Florence had much evidence to the contrary. New reforms were now going through in India.

She was feeling a great deal better – but her life still revolved around her work. She would not see anyone who called without an appointment.

In her lifetime she had seen incredible changes in medicine – chloroform, ether, Lister's work with antiseptics, Pasteur's revelations regarding germs. Hospitals had been transformed. Her life and work seemed a bridge between two centuries. Even when she was seventy-three she prepared a lecture on Sick Nursing and Health Nursing to be read at the Chicago Exhibition of Women's Work. Her store of knowledge, founded on a lifetime of research and experience, was formidable.

The world of Scutari seemed light-years away.

Old age

After her stormy life Florence Nightingale's old age was happy and peaceful. She was surrounded by people she loved and who loved her. Her rewards had come late, but they had come at last.

She continued to keep a close eye on the management of her household; she had a staff of five, not including her personal maid and the elderly messenger who delivered notes and letters for her all

over London. The house was, of course, immaculate and organized down to the minute. There were always fresh flowers in every vase, and the cleanest, crispest linen on Miss Nightingale's bed. She also continued to delight in interviewing girls who wanted to become nurses, enjoying their comments, and analyzing their characters.

She and Parthe now put aside their long-standing differences. Florence nursed Parthe through the illnesses of her final years, her patience never failing despite Parthe's continued awkwardness.

After Parthe's death in 1890 Florence, undaunted by the advancing years, embarked on a scheme to train Health Visitors. And she continued to write letters, interfering in the best possible way in matters of public concern.

Her eyes began to fail and she was nearly blind, but otherwise in better health than she'd enjoyed for years. She was cheerful and it showed in her face, a rounder, plumper, milder face than the stern, haggard look of forty years earlier. She no longer wrote despairingly about life, no longer hoped to die. "There is so much to live for," she wrote in 1895. "I have lost much in failures and disappointments, as well as in grief but, do you know, life is more precious to me now in my old age."

A fitting memorial

Gradually, quietly, the indefatigable Miss Nightingale faded. The body that had been through so much, that had withstood the hardships of war in the Crimea and innumerable diseases, did not give up easily. By 1901 she could see nothing at all. The children of cousins came and read aloud to her. And she in turn recited famous poems, or sang to them in a voice almost as sweet as it had been in those far-off days in Italy.

Eventually her mind clouded altogether – by 1906 the household staff had to inform the India Office that there was no longer any point in sending Miss Nightingale papers on sanitary matters.

In November 1907, King Edward VII awarded Florence Nightingale the Order of Merit – the first time it was ever bestowed on a woman. The Order

"Though I am known as the founder of the Red Cross and the originator of the Convention of Geneva, it is to an Englishwoman that all the honour of that Convention is due. What inspired me to go to Italy during the war of 1859 was the work of Miss Florence Nightingale in the Crimea."

Henry Dunant

was delivered by a representative of the King to her house in London, but Florence scarcely understood what was happening. After murmuring, "Too kind, too kind" she dropped back to sleep.

In 1909 the Poor Law Report laid down recommendations which would ensure that all the reforms Florence had supported would be carried out. Then in May 1910 came the Jubilee of the Nightingale Training School for Nurses and a meeting was held at New York's Carnegie Hall to mark the occasion. By now, more than a thousand training schools had been set up in the United States alone and Florence's achievements were acclaimed at the meeting.

But Florence was unaware of any of this. She grew weaker and weaker and on August 13, 1910, at the age of ninety, she fell asleep – and did not wake again.

According to her own wishes, Florence was buried very quietly and without pomp near the family's home at Embley, her coffin carried by six sergeants of the British Army.

Only a small cross marks her grave.

"F.N. Born 1820. Died 1910."

She wanted no greater memorial.

Busload after busload of nurses made their way to pay tribute to Florence Nightingale at her funeral in 1910: She had shown herself, beyond doubt, to be one of the most influential, best-loved people of her time.

Glossary

Anaesthetic: a pain-suppressing drug which causes a person to lose consciousness, so that a doctor can operate.

Anglican: a member of the Church of England, under the authority of the Archbishop of Canterbury.

Barracks: a large building where soldiers live. In those days, usually with little or no *sanitation* and very unhealthy.

Catholic: a member of the Church of Rome, that is under the authority of the Pope. In Florence's time, relations between Rome and the Anglican Church hardly existed; Anglicans and Catholics viewed each other with great distrust.

Cholera: a serious stomach infection, caused by drinking or cooking with polluted water. Its main symptoms are stomach cramps, diarrhoea and vomiting. In Florence's time, it was usually fatal.

Commission, Royal: an official government enquiry set up by royal *warrant* to investigate either how laws work or particular areas of social, educational or other concern. A Commission is given firm lines of reference and must produce a report to the government on what changes are needed and how they should be achieved.

Crimean War: Fought between 1854 and 1856 by Great Britain, Sardinia, France and Turkey against the Empire of Russia. Russia was trying to expand her territory around the Black Sea at the expense of Turkey. Most of the fighting took place near Varna in what is now Bulgaria and in the Crimean peninsula.

Dysentery: another serious stomach disease, caused by drinking infected water. Its chief symptom is diarrhoea which includes blood or mucus (a slimy fluid).

Epidemic: an outbreak of an infectious disease which spreads very rapidly.

Parthenope: a character from the Greek myths. She was one of the sirens (a little like mermaids) who drowned herself when one Greek hero managed to escape the lure of their song. It was said her body was washed ashore at Naples, which was where Florence's sister was born.

Peninsula: a piece of land which is almost an island. It is connected to the mainland by a narrow strip of land known as an isthmus.

Protestant: Christians who do not acknowledge the authority of the Pope. Usually they belong to churches which base their worship on the systems originated by Martin Luther or John Calvin.

Sanitation: Nowadays understood to relate mostly to drainage systems and sewage, in Florence's time it meant anything to do with public health. The adjective is "sanitary", so a "Sanitary Commission" is one dealing with public health concerns.

Statistics: a collection of facts and figures about a particular topic which allows you to get an overall view of the topic. Florence was brilliant at collecting and remembering facts and figures about health and hospitals and was one of the first people in the world to do so.

Typhus: a highly-infectious fever, spread by insect bites. Its main symptoms are a high temperature, purple spots on the skin and dreadful headaches.

Vermin: any small animal or insect which is a nuisance to humans. This can range from rats and mice which eat and pollute our food to fleas, lice and other insects that live off human blood. Many of these can infect humans with diseases. They will occur anywhere where washing and laundry facilities are lacking.

Victorian: Queen Victoria reigned in Great Britain from 1838 to 1901. This period has many typical ideas, attitudes, styles and interests which are generally described by the word "Victorian".

Warrant: a document which authorizes a person or a group to do something. Royal Warrants are signed by the Monarch.

Workhouse: Up to the 1930s every town or rural district in Great Britain had a series of buildings where people who had no money were put to work in return for food and lodging. In Florence's day, because they were separated by sex, any family "sent to the workhouse" was split up and not allowed to meet.

Further Reading

Bull, Angela: *Florence Nightingale* (London: Hamish Hamilton, 1985)

Connor, Edwina: *A Child in Victorian London* (London: Wayland, 1986)

Davey, Cyril: *Florence Nightingale – the Lady with the Lamp* (London: Lutterworth Press, 1956)

Holland, Lesley: *Working in a Hospital* (London: Batsford, 1983)

Hodgson, Pat: *Nursing* [Working Lives series] (London: Batsford, 1986)

Huxley, Elspeth: *Florence Nightingale* (London: Weidenfeld & Nicholson, 1975)

Masson, Madeleine: *A Pictorial History of Nursing* (London: Hamlyn, 1985)

Quennell, Marjorie and C.H.B.: *Everyday Things in England 1851-1914* (London: Batsford, 1956)

Rawcliffe, Michael: *Finding Out about Victorian Social Reformers* (London: Batsford, 1987)

Rose, Lionel: *Health & Hygiene* [Past-into-Present series] (London: Batsford, 1986)

Stewart, Anne: *The Ambulance-Woman* (London: Hamish Hamilton, 1985)

——: *The Doctor* (London: Hamish Hamilton, 1985)

Woodham-Smith, Cecil: *Florence Nightingale* (London: Constable, 1951) [This is a heavy reference book but very important as it is by far the best adult biography.]

Important Dates

1820   May 12: Florence Nightingale born in Florence, Italy.

1837   Feb 7: Florence is "called" to the service of others.

1844   Florence realizes her vocation is with the sick in hospital.

1845   Florence tries to train at the Salisbury Infirmary, but family opposition defeats her.

1846-53 Florence studies hospitals and sanitation in secret.

1847   Florence goes to Rome after an illness. She meets Sidney Herbert and his wife.

1849   Richard Monckton Milnes proposes to Florence. In November, Florence is on the brink of a nervous breakdown. The Bracebridges take her to Egypt and Greece.

1850   July: The Bracebridges arrange for her to visit Kaiserswerth for two weeks.

1851   July: Florence finally goes to work at Kaiserswerth for three months. Her father is won over to her goal of nursing.

1853   Apr: Florence accepts the post of Superintendent at a private London hospital. Her father agrees to make her an allowance.

1854   Britain, France and Turkey declare war on Russia.
        Aug: During a cholera epidemic, Florence nurses at London's Middlesex Hospital as a volunteer.
        Sept: Allied armies land in the Crimea.
        Oct 15: Sidney Herbert (Secretary at War) asks Florence to lead a party of nurses to Scutari.
        Nov 5: The party arrives at the Barrack Hospital in Scutari.
        Dec: The Army's supply organization has broken down totally. Florence is supplying the whole Army medical service.

1855   Florence drafts proposals for improving the Army supply and medical provision, despite working up to twenty hours a day.
        May 10: Florence collapses with Crimea fever.
        Nov 29: In Britain, the Nightingale Fund is launched.

1856   April 29: Peace declared
        July 16: The last patient leaves Scutari hospital.
        July 28: Florence returns to England and works to reform the health administration of the army.
        Sept: She meets Queen Victoria and asks for a Royal Commission on Army medical organization.

1857   May 5: Warrant for Royal Sanitary Commission on the Health of the Army issued. Florence works endlessly. She is also writing her *Notes on Matters affecting the Health, Efficiency and Hospital Administration of the British Army.*

1858   Parthe marries Sir Harry Verney.
        Dec: Florence publishes a popular version of her *Notes.*

1859   May: Warrant setting up the Indian Sanitary Commission issued. *Notes on Hospitals* published to acclaim.
        Dec: *Notes on Nursing* published.

1860	June 24: Nightingale Training School for Nurses opens.
1861	Aug 2: Herbert dies. Florence collapses from grief. First training school for district nurses set up in Liverpool. The Nightingale Training School for Midwives opens at King's College Hospital.
1862-7	Florence drafts cost-accounting system for Army Medical Services. She becomes the War Office's No. 1 adviser on health, drafting minutes, warrants and regulations.
1864	Jan: Florence (with others) completes her *Suggestions in regard to Sanitary Works required for the Improvement of Indian Stations*. Feb: Florence recruits nurses to work at Liverpool Workhouse Infirmary.
1865	Feb: Florence starts work on workhouse administration reform.
1866	Nov: Florence writes and submits paper on workhouse reform to a general government inquiry.
1867	Mar: Metropolitan Poor Act passed. June: Following closure of Nightingale Midwife Training School because of an epidemic, Florence starts collecting statistics on deaths in childbirth. This takes three years.
1870	July: During the Franco-Prussian War, the British Red Cross Society is founded. Florence appeals for funds. She later receives medals from both sides for her work.
1872	July: Florence visits her family; she feels she must help as her parents can no longer cope.
1873	Apr-May: Florence and a surgeon of St. Thomas's draw up a new plan of instruction for the Nightingale School. She becomes much more closely involved with the students.
1874	Jan 10: Florence's father dies. She has to nurse her mother.
1876	Florence writes to *The Times* about district nursing. Reprinted, the pamphlet goes into two editions.
1877-9	Throughout 1877 there is a serious famine in India. In 1878-9, Florence campaigns for irrigation and for the truth about the famine, writing endless articles and letters.
1880	Feb 2: Her mother dies. Apr: Florence spends the next four years campaigning for reforms in India.
1883	Parthe is seriously ill; Florence takes charge.
1887	India: Land reform and irrigation schemes are promoted; female nurses are allowed in military hospitals and many military welfare schemes begin.
1890	May: Parthenope dies.
1896	Florence never leaves her bedroom again.
1901	Florence's eyesight fails totally: she is often in a coma.
1907	Edward VII awards her the Order of Merit, the first ever to a woman.
1910	Aug 13: Florence dies in her sleep.

Index